What's the Deal with Teens and Time Management?

LESLIE JOSEL

To my husband, Wayne, my true partner in every way.

And to Maddie and Eli who allow me to hone my organizing skills every day.

And a special dedication to my students and their families, who continue to inspire and teach me each day.

Contents

INTRODUCTION

Why Write a Book on
Teens and Time Management?

Let me take you back eleven years.

When my son Eli was five, he was diagnosed with ADHD and executive dysfunction. Wanting to do everything I could to untangle his world, I did massive amounts of research. I read articles, attended conferences, sought out experts. Uncovering ways to get and keep my son organized and teach him time management skills became my passion...and my business. (We'll get to that!) I learned systems and strategies that could be used to bring some order to the chaos at home and school. But the most effective "research" I did was to talk to parents like me to learn from their experiences, share information and provide support.

After reorganizing my home top to bottom, a dear therapist friend of mine came to visit. She looked around my home and said, "I have a patient you have to do this for; a mom with three boys under the age of 10."

So off I went to transform this desperate mom's home and life. We created "homes" for all their belongings, took doors off closets so her children could "see" what they owned, removed dressers from rooms and replaced them with clear bins and hooks. We put time management strategies into place. Out went useless checklists and up went eye-catching directions. Analog clocks were hung; schedules firmed up, launching pads created and on it went. After 10 hours (Yes, I am that crazy!), I had helped this sweet woman transform her chaotic and unhappy house into a calm and orderly home. Within the next two weeks, I received four phone calls from her friends asking for my help. I turned to my husband and said, "I don't do this for a living!" And his response? "Well, you do now." And so, my company, "Order Out of Chaos®" was born.

Fast forward 11 years and boy have things changed. What was once a personal mission and then a whim of a business idea has now grown into a thriving full-service professional organizing company specializing in chronic disorganization. Now, before you laugh and think that "professional organizers" are all about labeling kitchen shelves or purchasing the best sports equipment holder for the garage, you are wrong. Way wrong. The work we do is so much more than that.

"Order Out of Chaos®" offers organizing, time management and coaching services; family education, and ADHD resources as well as classes, educational videos and products to hundreds of families and their students—both mainstream and those with learning differences. Our mission is to bring peace, sanity and hope, as well as personalized organizing and time management systems and structure, to families with true struggles.

For some, these struggles leave them with little hope and great despair.

I regularly travel the country presenting to parents, students, and teachers on issues surrounding teens today. Over the years, the single most requested subject I am asked to speak on or parents are concerned about is time management, an issue filled with emotion, anxiety, and confusion. Not a day goes by that I am not speaking, writing, emailing, coaching, or talking on this subject. Having developed an arsenal of what I call "The Triple Ts"—tips, tools and techniques—for teens and time management (and for parents!), it was time to write a book.

My goal in writing this book is simply to provide support and guidance for parents looking to help their teens understand, develop and implement time management skills. And in doing so, I've included a LOT of information. So before you dive in I wanted to remind you of a few things: The book is meant as a guide; one to pick up again and again whether to learn a new set of skills or just for a refresher course. Some of the strategies will hit home immediately; others you will dismiss outright. Some of the methods are meant for younger teens; others for older. To get the most out of the book, it is most important for you to go through it at your own pace, on your own time and in your own way.

So now that I've given you some pointers and things to do, here's what I DON'T want you to do:

- Stress out. As parents, we want to do EVERYTHING for our children. And since I have written a book with tons of strategies and suggestions, some will feel that they have to do all of them....and at the same time. That could not be further from the truth. The goal here is NOT to have you do everything at once, think you are not doing enough, or worse, everything wrong.

- Try to absorb everything at once and immediately implement every single strategy discussed here. After reading through the book (or looking at the Table of Contents), start with one area or aspect of your teen's school or home life that you'd like to work on most, such as the morning routine or procrastination, and focus on that chapter. Then find the tips and strategies in that chapter that resonate with you and your teen. Remember, the goal is to try a little at a time and keep it manageable—for both you and your teen!

- Think these solutions are intended to be quick fixes. This process will take effort and patience. If you see they are working, great. And if they are not working, no worries. Move on. If all you do is enable your teen to regularly and effectively use one specific time management skill, you should consider that a victory since that one, newly-developed skill could make all the difference in the world and will most likely facilitate the learning of another.

- Be on a schedule. When it comes to developing time management skills, there is no clock or calendar. In other words, I can't tell you how long it will be until you see progress. For some, a particular strategy may bring fast results. For others, it may take months of work before your teen will effectively use one of these techniques. There are simply too many variables at play. But as I've seen in my work with my clients—and with my son, Eli—parents tend to have an innate sense of whether something will work with their teen and how long it may take for them to grab on.

And speaking of Eli, you may be wondering about his time management skills. (I get asked that question a lot too!) He's "a third, a third and a third" kind of teen! What do I mean? A third of his time management skills were taught by me, a third he rejected outright and a third he developed on his own. If you think about it, isn't that the way it's supposed to be? But after all these years of living with me, Eli truly recognizes the importance of learning and developing these skills and is much more open to using them. Home Run!

So don't get discouraged. Trust yourself and your teen, keep working at it and try different approaches until you find what works. Go slow. Keep throwing things up against the wall and see what sticks. As I have come to learn, working with teens on time management skills is truly a work in progress. So let's get started.

CHAPTER 1

Can I Really Help My Teen Develop Time Management Skills?

Time management is a challenge for everyone, but it is a particularly daunting challenge for middle and high school students. There is an expectation that at their age they should be independent and know how to get things done on their own. In today's fast-paced culture, effective time-management skills are essential to succeed at home, in school, and in life.

However, between homework, school, afterschool activities, family, friends, jobs, and more, teens often find that their time is truly NOT their own. If you add in the fact that they often lack the tools to understand how to prioritize, initiate, or even organize their belongings, maybe it's a little unrealistic for parents to expect their teenagers to instinctively know how to manage time.

Because of this, it's important for parents to help their teens master basic time management strategies as it will enable their future success.

Many parents I work with ask me "Is it even possible to teach this stuff?" My answer is always an emphatic

"Yes! But **YOU** must have the right techniques, and even more so, the right mindset to do so." Here's what I mean:

Mindset #1:

Time Management is a Life Skill that Doesn't Come Naturally to Everyone. It Can be Learned.

Learning to effectively manage one's time requires learning new behaviors, developing unique strategies, as well as a great deal of patience. It is important to help your teen understand that just like any other muscle in the body, strengthening their time management "muscle" takes consistent training, proper exercise techniques, and the right equipment. In this way, I like to equate it to running a marathon.

As their time management "coach" you will want to help your teen identify their struggles so they can work to overcome them. The following are some of the things that teenagers might have trouble with:

- Getting homework done

- Understanding how much time a project will take them to complete

- Initiating activities or tasks

- Prioritizing assignments

- Procrastinating and motivation issues

- Keeping track of time

- Finishing work on time

Knowing which skills are essential for them to carry out their everyday tasks will help you to assist in the development of appropriate strategies and tools to help them make it to the finish line!

Mindset #2:

Instead of Focusing on Behavior, Focus on the Brain.

When a student struggles with time management, procrastinates over homework, has a hard time staying focused, or has difficulties organizing her binders or backpack, weak executive function skills may be at play.

What are "executive functions?"

The National Center of Learning Disabilities describes executive functions "*as a set of mental processes that helps us connect past experience with present action. We use executive functions when we perform such activities as planning, organizing, strategizing and paying attention to and remembering details.*"[1]

Simply stated, executive functions are what we use to get things done and how we remember to do them. They come into play anytime we perform even the simplest task or behavior.

A real life example that will help to explain the importance of executive functions is one that teenagers face often:

A student is given a long-term project and must plan out the time it will take to complete it according to a teacher's specifications. In order to do so, the teen needs organizing, time management, and self-regulating skills.

1 National Center for Learning Disabilities' Executive Function Fact Sheet found at http://www.ldonline.org/article/24880?theme=print.

A student who has difficulty with executive functions might:

- Not be able to break down the steps needed for a project.

- Have difficulty getting started or once he does, may not be sure how to prioritize the steps needed to complete the assignment.

- Have trouble collecting the resources and materials needed and not know how to sufficiently organize them.

- Set unrealistic deadlines to work on the project or set none at all.

- Not monitor her progress from beginning to end, running the risk of turning in the assignment late or not at all.

Lastly, many students will become so overwhelmed and frustrated by the enormity of the project that they will shut down completely and refuse to work on it.

Now, it is important to note that executive functions are not fully developed until a person is in their mid-20s. Some experts say they don't develop until even later. Because of the mismatch between the brain's ability and our culture's expectations of what teens should be able to do puts a tremendous amount of undue stress on our students and can affect their day-to-day performance.

Mindset #3:

It's Not About the Outcome, But How They Get There.

As parents, we all want our teens to be academically successful and get "good" grades. I get it! I have two students of my own, but how we define "academic success" should be unique to EACH teen, and more importantly, shouldn't be the primary focus at home. Time management and organizational strategies should be! When I work with a teen and she tells me she received a 95 on her latest exam or paper, I ask her how she got there, meaning how did she get herself to a place where she could perform so well. Here are a few examples of some of the questions that I ask to better ascertain the level at which a student should and could perform:

- Did you plan your studying around your other activities?

- Were you able to break the assignment down into manageable parts and not feel overwhelmed?

- Were your notes organized and easily accessible?

- Did you cram the night before or did you leave yourself ample time?

In the long run, the student who answered yes to most of these questions will be better off than peers with higher grades that answered no! Time and organizational skills are paramount for success in life. No one is going to remember what grade your teenager received on her Mesopotamia project in 8th grade. However, her college professor or boss will absolutely remember if she doesn't turn a paper in on time or meet a critical deadline.

Mindset #4:

Raise problem solvers, not direction followers.

The hardest parenting lesson I had to learn was to stop telling my children what to do.

That lesson took time and patience, neither of which I had in abundance, especially when my children were younger. For me, it was much easier to bark orders and commands then it was to let them figure things out on their own. Because of that, my children relied heavily on me to tell them where they needed to be, what they needed to do and even what they needed to bring. They had become expert direction followers.

I would walk in the door, and everyone would "line up" and the conversation would read something like: "Maddie, go get your tap shoes and grab your snack. We need to leave for dance in 15 minutes." "Eli, go change for fencing and don't forget a towel and your water bottle. Your ride will be here in 5." Harried and exhausted, I would keep my eye on the clock all the while grabbing items, packing bags, and worrying about getting them out the door on time. Then one day I realized it was time for them to take some ownership. However, in order for them to be able to do that, I would need to change what I did.

So how did I change my behavior? I talked less (or more accurately I directed less) and questioned more. Rather than listening to what I said and doing it, my kids needed to listen to the question I asked, think about it and formulate a response. By talking less and questioning more, I enabled them (actually compelled them) to engage and participate in what they were doing. Most importantly, I began asking the right questions, and you can too.

Use questions like:

"What's Your Plan...?"

I love this one because you can put almost anything at the end of it. "What's your plan after school?" "What's your plan before dinner?" For older teens, you can even ask, "What's your plan for studying for your two tests on Friday when you get home from your soccer game at 9:00pm on Thursday night." The list can go on and on.

The purpose of asking this question and in this manner is to help your teen to begin to develop a sense of time. I always say that for the most part teens live in two worlds—the "now" and the "not now". They have a very difficult time making the connection that what they have to do later in the day or even later that week or month, can affect what they need to do now.

This lack of "future awareness" is one of the hardest concepts to teach and one of the hardest to learn. It is the essence of true time management. In this way, this question is a wonderful and organic way for teens to begin to formulate routines and schedules and remember what they need to accomplish in the process.

"How Do You See Yourself?"

There are a lot of variations on this question, like **"What do you need to ..?"** or **"How should you..?"** These will work just as well, but the purpose of this question is to help your teen begin to build a visual checklist for what needs to be done and how to do it. Here are some more examples of this question alongside the "directions" they can replace:

- "What needs to be packed in your dance bag?" instead of, "Go get your dance shoes, bag, towel, and leotard."

- "How should you leave your bedroom in the morning before going to school?" instead of, "You need to make your bed and pick up your clothes before leaving."

- "What do you need to take with you to school each morning?" instead of, "Don't forget your back pack, cell phone, keys, lunch, etc."

- "When do we need to leave to get to school on time?" instead of, "We need to leave in 5 minutes to be on time."

By turning the tables and asking instead of telling, you are requiring your teens to do some planning of their own. Don't get discouraged if at the beginning you get a lot of "I don't knows."

Flipping that response around and asking "Well, what do you know?" is a great way to get the dialogue going. By building consistency and routines, getting your teen to pack a dance bag or get out the door in the morning with everything she needs will become as habit forming as brushing teeth or wearing a seat belt.

Mindset #5:

Everyone Learns Differently and Therefore Manages Time Differently

Have you ever wondered why your teen wasn't born with the same time management "gene" as you?

You're not alone.

How we process information, organize our thoughts, and lay down that learning is called our "learning style" and every individual, including teens, learns in a slightly different way. Learning styles start to crystallize during the middle school years and at that time; most teens tend to be stronger in one particular area over others. Because of this, the best thing you can do as a parent is to step back and observe what seems to be working well for your teen and build from there.

Since the early 1970s researchers have been studying individual learning styles and have adopted four modalities of learning:[2]

- **VISUAL** learners rely on what they see. They benefit from illustrations and visual presentations, are good readers and take copious notes. They respond best to instruction that includes reading, graphs and videos. They also learn by watching what you or others do.

- **AUDITORY** learners absorb information by listening. They remember best by verbalizing new information, like to read aloud, and can learn in a noisy environment. They benefit most from instruction based on discussion and questioning. For example, explaining each part of a process and how

2 Education.com Learning Modalities found at http://www.education.com/print/learning-modalities/.

each step should be done will help them remember information.

- **KINESTETIC** learners learn best by doing. They enjoy hands-on instruction, using manipulatives, role-playing, or building things. Touch and movement are critical for these learners to absorb information. They also remember what was done, not necessarily what was seen or heard. Therefore, it is important with these types of learners for them to TEACH you.

- **TACTILE** learners like to use their hands and fingers to learn. These students learn best by writing, drawing, and doodling. They tend to touch or feel objects when learning a new concept and illustrate what they have learned.

Children struggle when they try to learn in ways that aren't natural for them. Remember that there isn't one correct way to teach, just as there isn't one correct way to learn. Knowing and understanding your teen's learning style is crucial when helping them learn effective time management skills.

As we move on to practical examples for teaching your teen time management, it is important to keep these learning styles in mind and recognize which ones your teen tends to utilize most. Otherwise, you will find yourself struggling and getting frustrated as you develop methods for your teen to manage time successfully.

CHAPTER 2

How Can I Get My Teen
To See Time?

By encouraging and helping your teen learn what he or she needs to develop good personal time management skills, you are also helping your teen become successful and independent. It might seem like an overwhelming process, but if you begin with the premise that most teens want to do well and succeed, then the journey should be a smooth one. Rather than lecture, your role is to guide and coach. Build their confidence and let them know they are in charge of the process. Here are some basic tools to get you started.

Review All Commitments

I can't stress this enough. Students need to manage so much in their lives, and they often don't have enough time to do it all. Sit down with your teen and go over everything on their schedule—both during and after school. Do they really need to play on three hockey teams? Belong to five clubs? Play tennis and perform in the school musical? Are they running from class to class without a free or lunch period? Even the best time management strategies won't magically allow your teen to squeeze in everything they want to do. A wise woman once told me "You can do everything you want, just not all at the same time!" And here is where your teen needs your guidance. I know it is hard to say no, but it is better to be truly involved in a few activities than just show up to many.

When discussing this with your teen make sure both of you fully understand what the time commitments are for each of their activities. I worked with a family recently whose high school daughter wanted to play field hockey. The parents immediately said yes, thinking the team aspect of the sport would be a wonderful experience for their daughter. They knew the practice and game schedules. However, they failed to take into account off-season training sessions, team dinners on game nights and countless school and fundraising events. These "extras" added major stress to their daughter's schedule and the household too. So make sure you and your teen truly understand what may be involved with an activity and how it may impact all of the other commitments he or she has. Only then can you have a productive discussion.

Plan Weekly

In my home, my son and I hold bi-weekly meetings. With phones and planners in hand, we spend a few minutes at the beginning and in the middle of the week reviewing what needs to be accomplished for the week in terms of school assignments, afterschool activities, family events, etc., and then setting up a schedule accordingly. We keep these meetings quick and informal, but we include everything from upcoming tests and project dates to play rehearsals, doctors' appointments, and weekend activities. To avoid being a nag, I make sure I share my schedule too so he knows if he can count on me for a ride or needs to make alternate plans. By approaching our time together as a joint planning session, my son does not feel as if I'm being intrusive or critical.

Trust me when I say it took us a long time to get to this point! But by constantly reminding him that he needs to know if I am available on certain days makes him available to me! These weekly meetings also allow me to help him build time management skills by encouraging him to think forward and make a plan to accomplish what needs to get done. It also provides me an opportunity to offer critical support and encouragement.

Prioritize Activities

If your teen has her Orchestra concert and her best friend's birthday the day before the unit test in Chemistry, she is really going to be at a loss to know how to fit it all in. So how can you help? If you are holding meetings during the week like I mentioned above, then you will have seen this coming and can plan accordingly.

Here's how I would handle the above scenario:

First, I would explain to my teen that her Chemistry test is her first priority and she needs to plan on starting to review for the exam days in advance (more on that in Chapter 4). This will lighten her load the night before the test.

Remember our question, "What's Your Plan?" This is a perfect time to ask your teen how she will study for the Chemistry test if she doesn't get home from her concert until late the night before. The concert is a responsibility that your teen has to attend, so it is non-negotiable.

As for the birthday? Suggest celebrating over the weekend or decorating her friend's locker before school or giving her a small gift on the actual day. Figuring this all out takes time, but I promise that once your teen learns how to prioritize her schedule your need to be hands on will lessen.

Build Routines

Once a routine is established, a task or activity takes less time to do. While this sounds like a simple enough concept, it's one that teens constantly resist. Let's say you want your teen to make her bed every morning before going to school. You end up reminding her each morning; she goes running back to her room to make it and therefore, ends up being late getting out the door. Lots of time has been wasted, and you are frustrated and annoyed. If your teen gets into the habit of getting out of bed and making her bed then, she will be done in less than a minute. Try to stress that devoting one minute at the beginning of the morning will give her more time in the end. Not to mention that all that time wasted arguing will be gone!

Use Analog Clocks and Watches

By the time your child is in their teens they know how to tell time and were probably taught on a digital clock.

Unfortunately, a digital clock is not useful for teaching "time planning" as you can only see one aspect of time—the present.

Use an "old-fashioned" analog clock!

An analog clock, with its hands, lets you "see" time move and therefore where you stand in relation to the rest of the day. With an analog clock you can see present time (based on where the hands are when you look at them), elapsed time (based on where the hands were at the beginning of a period and where they are in the present) and future time (based on how far the hands need to move to get to a time in the future). These are the very building blocks of time management. **Seeing** elapsed and future time helps your teen **learn** about these concepts, and helps them better understand how long they spend on tasks and how much time they have before a deadline arrives.

So hang an analog clock in each room of the house that your student uses (Yes, even the bathroom!) so they can see the passing of time. Encourage your teen to wear an analog watch as well. I get a great deal of pushback on this point. Usually my students will reply that they don't need to wear one since they carry a cell phone. I point out that their phone is NOT a watch and is usually kept in either their pocket or backpack. Usually a cool, fun watch will do the trick!

Model Behavior

As we all know, when trying to impart lessons on our children, they learn better by watching then listening to us. So remember to "walk the walk!"

Make a point of mentioning when you are using effective time management techniques, such as when you help them with homework and prepare dinner at the same time, or when you get errands done in between dropping and picking them up. It's just as important to let them see you struggle and suffer consequences too.

I had a parent who would consistently model time planning by thinking aloud when she planned her own activities. She would say things like, "I have to pick up your dad at the train station at 6:30. It's 5:45 now and it takes me 10 minutes to get there. I should leave the house at 6:20 which gives me 35 minutes until I have to leave." The words "time management" don't have to be said. Just making your teen aware of how you get things done (or don't) can work its way into their subconscious and stay with them.

CHAPTER 3

What's "Time Sense" Got to Do with Time Management?

I could write a whole book on the importance of developing a time sense. The bottom line? In order to be successful at time management, you must know how long it takes to get things done. Having a time sense will help you establish routines, set limits, and learn to prioritize.

Estimating Time

When I first start working with a student, I gauge their time sense by asking them how long they think certain daily activities take them to do. The answer I usually get is that it takes about 20 minutes—*for everything!* It doesn't seem to matter whether I asked how long it takes them to walk the dog, make their lunch, or get to school. What this immediately means to me is that the student does not have a well-developed time sense.

You can do this test easily with your own teen. Start by casually asking them a series of questions similar to mine to see how in tune they are with how long things take. If everything seems to take about the same amount of time, their time sense could probably use some improvement.

To help your teen become more realistic about how long certain tasks take, have him write down estimates before doing them and then compare the estimates to the actual time it took to complete the task. The more he records and sees the difference between the estimated time and how long it actually takes to do something, the better he will become in developing a "time sense."

In addition, to improve their time sense, draw parallels between the time it takes to complete various activities by comparing an unknown period of time to something very familiar. Say something like, "It took you 30 minutes to read four chapters in your English book which is the same amount of time you spend watching a *Family Guy* episode." This will help your teen gain a better understanding of how long things take.

Mapping Time

"Visualizing" time is a big challenge for most. You can't see it or hold it in your hands which makes time a very difficult concept to understand. Learning to see time in a more tangible way can help to take its "invisibility" out of the equation. Here's one of my favorite student stories to illustrate my point:

I had a student, Michelle, who had a real challenge managing her time. She didn't understand why she didn't have enough time to get her homework done. She was a star swimmer and had lessons every day after school. She had to travel a ½ hour each way to get there.

When I first met with her, I asked her to "tell" me how she spent her time after school. She explained "I get out of school at 2:45 and have swim practice every day at 5:00pm. So I have about two hours to get my homework done before my lesson."

Now, I knew that was an unrealistic estimation of her time. However, I also knew that if I simply "told" her this, it would be hard for her to grasp. The point I was making would be more realistic to her if she could "see" how her time was actually spent.

So, I had Michelle keep an accurate account of how she spent her time for the week. It went something like this:

School over	**2:45**
Leave school to go home	**3:00**
Arrive home/eat snack	**3:15**
Walk dog	**3:30**
Change for swimming	**3:45**
Homework	**4:00**
Leave for swimming	**4:30**

Those two hours of homework time that Michelle told me about was now down to 30 minutes! We made some adjustments to Michelle's afterschool schedule so she would have more time to get started on assignments.

The point here is that to get an idea of where your time goes, you need to actually see it. So to get older teens like Michelle to see their time, I have them map it by tracking how they spend their time over the course of a week or two. This is something you can easily do at home.

Your teen can create a blank schedule grid on the computer or simply copy the one I've provided. First, block out their non-negotiable time, such as the time that is spent in school. However, if they have any free periods during the course of the day make sure they mark those on the sheet. Next, fill in afterschool activities and other commitments that are already planned. Now have your teen accurately record how the rest of the time is spent that week by recording activities in roughly ½ hour increments.

After the week is over, you and your teen should review the map. Ask if anything was surprising, such as something that took a lot more time than expected or whether there was free time in spots he didn't expect. Use his answers as a starting point for a discussion. Again, the map isn't intended as a solution, but as a tool to help your teen visualize time in order to develop a "time sense."

You can go to www.orderoochaos.com to print the Time Map in PDF format.

Time Map

	Mon	Tue	Wed	Thu	Fri	Sat	Sun
Wake							
8:00							
8:30							
9:00							
9:30							
10:00							
10:30							
11:00							
11:30							
12:00							
12:30							
1:00							
1:30							
2:00							
2:30							
3:00							
3:30							
4:00							
4:30							
5:00							
5:30							
6:00							
6:30							
7:00							
7:30							
8:00							
8:30							
9:00							
9:30							
10:00							
10:30							
11:00							
11:30							
Sleep							

CHAPTER 4

How Can I Help My Teen Better Plan Time?

A time map is a wonderful way to help a student visualize how they have spent their time. A proper academic planner helps students visualize what's ahead to enable them to plan for and manage what they need to do and *when they have the time to do it*. Using an academic planner will also help your teen stay on track. I can't overestimate the importance of a planner.

Remember that all planners are NOT created equal. Many planners, especially the ones given to students by schools, are glorified "to-do" lists and don't allow students to see their school, afterschool, evening and weekend lives as a whole. They just give students a place to record homework assignments. Here is a list of my "must haves" for an effective planner:

Features for the Perfect Planner

- The planner follows the school year (that is, it starts in August and ends in July) rather than the calendar year. Planners that follow the calendar year aren't suitable for students. Look for one that says, "Academic Planner" or "School Planner".

- It has a customizable subject index where students can write their class subjects only once. This feature will eliminate forgetfulness and frustration. Make sure the planner also comes with ample subject boxes, so there is room to write all their classes. I recommend one that has at least seven!

- The planner is set up as a grid system so they can see their week (and weekends!) at a glance. Weekly planner pages should line up with the index on a subject-by-subject basis, creating an easy and natural method for students to record and review their weekly schedules.

- Days of the week are listed horizontally across the planner. This makes recording entries simple and allows students to quickly see assignments and due dates and creates continuity critical to developing time management skills.

- The planner includes space to enter after-school activities and weekend commitments. **This is the KEY ingredient in planning their time to get work done.** Once they enter all their activities and commitments, scheduled and available blocks of time will naturally appear. Your student can now use those available time blocks to plan his or her weekly workload, facilitating weekly time management and planning strategies.

- There must be writing spaces that are large enough to record all the critical details of homework assignments and projects. Unfortunately, most planners on the market do not, which forces students to either severely "edit" the information they write down, write in short-hand or illegibly, leading to confusion when the planner is later opened for reference.

- Monthly calendar views are essential for long range planning as well as recording vacation and school holidays.

- Finally, a planner with an ample note section, preferably before each month, will help your student track both personal and school to-dos.

Paper Planner Pointers

In addition to making sure the planner your student uses is structured to facilitate time management, you also need to make sure your student *uses* it properly to help manage time. Here are a few pointers to keep your student on track when using a planner:

- Have your teen list all their subjects in the index. Most of my students prefer listing them in the order of their day.

- Make sure to include a row in the planner for **"Organizing"** so that your teen can plan locker, knapsack, and binder clean outs. Maintenance is key to getting AND staying organized.

- Have your teen record all after school activities, weekend commitments, and even plans with friends in the planner so he can see their available blocks of time to get things done. This will allow him to know what needs to be done AND when there is time to do it.

- All long term assignments and tests should be written down in every class, both on the day assigned AND on the day they are due. Some of my students write important assignments **VERTICALLY** for due dates to truly stand out.

- I encourage students to write "no homework" if none has been assigned to insure that they have not forgotten to record an assignment.

- Give sticky notes to your teen to remind her about an important assignment due or an upcoming school event. Different colors and sizes can be an extra reminder tool (e.g. large yellow for projects and papers, small blue for afterschool events, etc.)

- To build time awareness, have your teen enter the amount of time spent on each assignment right in the planner. This will provide him with an organic record of time spent on various tasks.

- Have your student mark the current page and week with a binder clip or use a page marker. This will cut down on those extra page-flips. Keep a pen in the planner also to avoid hunting for one during class.

- Make sure the planner is always handy and accessible. Suggest the front pockets of your teen's backpack or a large ring binder that she uses regularly.

Wall Calendars

In addition to using a planner, some students like having a wall calendar to give them a quick visual overview of their month to see upcoming events, due dates and holidays. Hang it on the wall over a desk or in the kitchen—make sure it is in full view!

I once had a client who kept her wall calendar on top of her desk. She never saw it as papers and books were piled on top of it!

Paper vs. Electronic

This is a tough call as I am a paper planner girl. I find that the most effective planner is organized for weekly and monthly views. This gives students the big picture, the sum of all the moving parts and I simply don't find that with electronic versions. It's worth noting that whenever we write information down it helps us to commit it to memory. So, when starting out with a planner, I encourage my students to begin with a paper one.

That said, not all students want or like a paper planner (Remember Mindset #5?). If that's the case, then I suggest they use an electronic version. While not my favorite way to develop true time management skills, I recognize the need to start somewhere. I would always prefer my students to get into the habit of recording their homework on an electronic device rather than not writing anything down at all.

So what about that student who refuses to write anything down or use anything at all? I'm sure you've heard the "I don't need to write it down, I can remember," or "It's a waste of time and too difficult to use," explanations. Listing the benefits of writing in a planner just doesn't work for these students.

I can't stress enough the importance of using a planner though!

One professor I know actually included it in her supply list and made it a mandatory requirement for her college class to stress its importance. She even went so far as to predict that those students that refused to use the planner would fail her course. And she was right.

As tempting as it may be to lay down the planner law and demand your teen use one, resist the idea. Like all systems, the planner will only be effective if your teen is willing to use it. Instead, start small and build slowly. Maybe they would prefer to snap a photo of their assignments or check the teacher's online website? Work with your teen to tap into a system that will work for them. Writing down homework is a habit, and like all habits it must be established over time.

Long Term Projects

If your student is tackling a long term project, begin by working with him to outline the goal of the project and list all the steps required. **(Or use our Project Planning Guide included in this chapter.)**

Make sure each task is manageable and specific. After all, it is much easier to write one paragraph every afternoon than it is to complete the entire research paper in one night. Here are some steps to follow when planning a long term project:

Planning Guidelines

- Make an outline of the steps necessary to complete the assignment. For written reports, for instance, the steps might include taking notes, generating an outline, writing the introduction, the sections of the report and the summary, preparing a bibliography, drawing any necessary maps and charts, proofreading, and preparing the final draft.

- Estimate how much time your student will need to finish each step and then work backwards from the due date. Always build in extra padding! I normally tack on an extra 25% as a buffer against false starts, interruptions and unanticipated problems.

- Assign deadlines for completing each step and record them in the planner. Plan on having your teen finish two days in advance of the due date. Being able to incorporate long term projects into their daily studying routine is essential for building their time management muscle!

- Include time for hidden tasks such as purchasing materials, going to a museum, proofreading drafts, etc.

- Encourage your teen to use free periods and study halls to work on their projects. Using down time during school breaks or conference days to get a jump start on their long term assignments and projects is a great way to take the pressure off.

> Use this guide when assigned a long term project or paper that has multiple steps.

PROJECT NAME: _____ DUE DATE: _____

What do you need to answer?

THESIS/QUESTION: _____

_____

_____

_____

What criteria are required (e.g., number of pages, types of sources, style, font, etc.)?

GUIDELINES: _____

_____

_____

_____

What steps are needed to complete the project?

#	STEPS	SET DEADLINE

Don't forget to enter your dates in your planner.

What tools are needed?

MATERIALS:	
INFORMATION:	
RESOURCES:	

You can go to www.orderoochaos.com to print the Project Planning Guide in PDF format.

CHAPTER 5

Are There Homework Strategies that Work?

I hate homework—but not for the reasons that you may think. I'm all for homework that reinforces lessons taught in school, projects that can really speak to a student's creativity and learning styles, and assignments that challenge a student to be a critical thinker and problem solver.

What I hate about homework is two-fold.

First, most homework assignments place more emphasis on content rather than process (Remember Mindset #3?). And second, because of that emphasis, students generally think that all that is needed to "successfully" deal with homework is to do what is asked of them. And, this is where the way that homework is assigned and approached by students falls short and an opportunity to learn lifelong skills is missed.

Let me explain: Ask any student if they give any thought to how they will tackle their evening homework, and I assure you their answer will be that they just sit down and do it. Juggling homework with everything else a teen has to do is not easy. Knowing what their best methods are to get homework done in an effective manner is even harder.

And, unfortunately, parents don't always know how to help here. Parents generally have strong opinions about how teens should do their homework. Maybe you think your teen should do their homework right after school. Maybe you think good study habits mean teens should study in the same place every day. Maybe you think that they should sit still until all their work is done.

Well, parents aren't always right! A lot of new research shows that the old ways of doing homework may not always be the best ways. As we learned in the first chapter, kids learn differently and therefore study best in different ways.

Students (and their parents) need to understand and appreciate that everyone has individual homework preferences and personalities—or what I call a **"Personal Homework Profile"**—and students need to learn how to tap into it to create a more holistic approach to get their work done.

Creating a Personal Homework Profile

A Personal Homework Profile takes the whole teen into account. This does not need to be a formal process. Think of it as just a guide to help you uncover your teen's best practices. Here are a just a few questions to get you and your teen started.

- What time is best for them to start homework?

- What is their energy level immediately after school?

- Do they prefer working in a noisy or calm environment?

- What type of snacks do they eat?

- Can they work fast and furious or do they need constant breaks to accomplish their work?

- Do they need music to keep them on task or does background noise work better?

Bottom line? Homework is the last thing your teen wants to be doing. So if we help them create a profile that taps into their strengths and needs we can provide them with tools and resources that will maximize their time management muscle.

How Do I Find My Teen's Prime Time?

I get asked this question a lot. And there is no right answer. However, the expectation that your student needs to start homework immediately after school is indeed old school...for some. There are those students who want and need to start their homework right away. That was my daughter, Maddie. When she was in middle school she would come straight home, not even take off her coat and go straight to her room to begin working. This strategy worked for her for one primary reason: Her afterschool activities were in the early evenings and she preferred to leave for them knowing her work was completed. That mindset was motivating, and a stress reliever for her.

However, starting homework right after school for many is ineffective and in some ways counterproductive.

Take my client Jake, a high school freshman. When Jake's mom first called me she was concerned that Jake had little to no time management skills. She explained further that it took Jake "hours" to get what little homework he had done. As I dove deeper into Jake's afterschool routine and homework habits, I found that Jake was beginning his homework immediately upon arriving home. His mom had put this rule in place in order to limit the amount of screen time Jake had afterschool. (I am sure we can all relate.) But Jake couldn't focus on his work. He would get up, walk around, eat, and find a million other reasons not to get started.

There can be many reasons for this type of procrastination (and we delve deeper in Chapter 6). So in discussing the situation with his mother, I asked what I think is a very important question and not one asked often enough. What was Jake's energy level like when she picked him up after school? Was he chatty? Happy? High energy? Or was he non-communicative, exhausted, wrung out? Her reply was, to me, very telling. "He doesn't say a word when he gets in the car. He just has nothing left in him by the end of the day." Now granted there were more things at play here that needed to be addressed. But in terms of dealing with Jake's homework issues, giving him some much needed down time immediately after school so he could "refuel his engine" and pushing his homework start time back, enabled Jake to better focus and attend, work more effectively and finish his homework at an appropriate time.

Does My Teen Need to Move Around Before She Works?

Yes! Each and every day more and more research comes out proving that movement and exercise have multiple benefits for learning and focus. And not just for kids! Just recently, an article was published in the September 2014 issue of *Pediatrics*,[3] on the importance of exercise on school success. Those students that participated daily in after-school activities during which they performed about 30 minutes of aerobic exercise were able to resist distraction, multitask and remember and use information. We know that movement helps lay down learning. Whether it's shooting baskets in the backyard or running up and down steps in your home get your teen up before they sit down!

Where Should My Teen Do His Homework?

Raise your hand if you think your teen needs to study at a desk…in his room…with his door closed.

I thought so! You're not alone. Most parents feel this is the optimum environment for their teens to work.

Again, for some it is. But for most, the bedroom is the least effective place in the house to get homework done. So before you go out and invest in that new desk for your teen, let me tell you one of my favorite client stories.

I met Randy when he was in 10th grade. Again, the call came in from his mother concerned that Randy had no time management skills and couldn't get his homework done. During homework time, Randy opted to

3 "How Exercise Can Boost Young Brains" found at http://well.blogs.nytimes.com/2014/10/08/how-exercise-can-boost-the-childs-brain/.

wander the house in search of his three younger siblings. A noisy bunch, his mom would redirect Randy back to his bedroom where it was quiet so he could work.

I headed straight to Randy's room on my initial site visit. A beautiful room on the third floor of their home, it was extremely quiet and secluded from the remainder of the house. I asked Randy why he didn't like doing his homework in his room. Interestingly, Randy found the silence upstairs too quiet and isolating to concentrate. So he gravitated to the downstairs noise where the goings-on helped him feel connected so he could relax and focus.

We brainstormed some ideas and this is what we came up with: Randy would do his homework on the kitchen table in the middle of all the hubbub. We purchased an inexpensive table top presentation board that he could place on top of the kitchen table to give him some privacy. In addition, he could either wear earplugs or listen to light music to drown out some of the noise but his siblings did not have to change their behavior. Their only rule was that they were to ignore their brother. With some other tweaks made, Randy was able to stay focused, attend to his homework and raise his grades.

The right location will truly depend on your child and the culture of your family. Some teens do best at a desk in their bedroom. It is a quiet location, away from the family noise. Other teens (like Randy) can feel isolated or become too distracted by the things they keep in their bedroom and do better at a place removed from those distractions, like the dining room table. Some need to work by themselves. Others need to have parents or family members nearby to help keep them on task and to answer questions when problems arise.

Ask your child where the best place is to work. You will be surprised that most teens can tell you exactly what environment works best for them. They just need help in creating the optimum situation.

Homework Games

What about the student that needs to move around and can't sit in one place to do homework? Let me introduce you to Rachel.

Rachel was one of my favorite students as she kept me on my toes. She bored easily and therefore ideas and strategies needed to be fun and full of energy for her to get excited about them. She also needed to move around a lot to focus. Calling on the teachings in Roland Rotz' groundbreaking book, "Fidget to Focus: Outwit Your Boredom", I took some of the initial principles of learning and movement and created some fun homework games for Rachel to try.

Hide the Homework. When Rachel came home from school, I had her gather all her books, supplies and homework for the evening and separate them into piles by subject on the kitchen table. Then without her looking, I hid her homework in various locations around her house. That first day, Science went into the bathtub in her bathroom; English vocabulary under the kitchen table; Math inside her mother's closet; and so on. Where ever she "found" her homework is where she had to do it. Needless to say, Rachel loved this game! By adding energy and fun into her daily homework routine, she was able to stay motivated and on-task.

Beat the Clock. As Rachel got older, we tried variations on the game as the initial methods no longer worked with her homework load. Working from the research that shifting subjects helps you stay focused[4], I introduced her and my older teens to **Beat the Clock.**

Similar to "Hide the Homework," I had each student separate their homework for the evening into piles by subject. They could place their homework wherever they wanted in their home. Some just made workstations around the dining room table while others placed different subjects in different rooms. The difference here was that they also set a timer to work on one subject at a time. (The age of the teen determined how long they worked, with older teens spending more time on each subject.) Once the timer went off, they finished whatever math problem, lab question, vocabulary sentence, etc.; they were working on and took a break. When they went back to work, they moved on to another subject.

The premise here is that by having students switch subjects continuously, they are less likely to drift off and lose focus. They might have to shift back and forth between assignments several times before the work is completed. However, giving your teen the mental break from one subject area by starting another is the key to being productive.

---

4 "6 Tips to Fight Distractions and Get Homework Done!" found at http://www.additudemag.com/adhd/article/print/8394. html.

Should My Teen Listen to Music While Studying?

There is an endless debate between scientists, researchers, teachers, and of course, parents on whether listening to music while doing homework is beneficial. Countless research studies have demonstrated the benefits of music in helping the brain activate. They say that music bolsters attention and focus. Others point out that certain types of music can be distracting and impede a student's recall and memorization.

The best description to help me understand why music is important to a student went like this: "Music is rhythm, and rhythm is structure, and that structure can help a student plan what to do next, anticipate and react as well as sooth and regulate the brain."[5]

But even with this logical explanation, when someone asks me about music and homework, I always give the same response: "It all depends on the student." Your teen might use music to help drown out distracting sounds around them. Others need it to get their adrenaline going to get motivated. Still others may get too focused on the music itself—singing along or playing air guitar—to do any work.

Your job is to help your teen know when the music is helping them focus and when it is distracting.

Make a thirty minute playlist. If my students find listening to music beneficial I suggest this technique for a variety of reasons.

---

5 "Music: Sound Medicine for ADHD" found at http://www.additudemag.com/adhd/article/print/9558.html.

First, playing the same playlist every time they sit down to work eliminates the distraction of changing songs on their desktop or portable device.

Second, since they will be listening to the same music over and over again, eventually the music will become background noise and they will, hopefully, focus on it less.

Third, the playlist can become a behavioral psychology tool—when the student hears the music on the playlist, he or she gets into work mode.

Lastly, the music can become a timekeeper for some. I have students that have been using playlists for so long that they know when they hear the Beatles they are 15 minutes in; when they hear Taylor Swift they know they are in the homestretch. Having the music create a time sense is a wonderful benefit to listening to music.

Can Certain Foods Help Provide Energy?

Whenever my son feels tired and needs energy before sitting down to work, we call upon protein-rich foods to be the magic elixir. It works so well we have come to chant, "All Hail, The Power of the Protein."

Now I am not a nutritionist, but I have read countless articles and heard dozens of professionals speak about how the right foods directly affect brain function. Research shows that protein, Omega-3 fatty acids, and even certain forms of glucose (such as those found in Gatorade or apple juice)[6] will give you energy, while your brain gets a boost.

---

6 "Brain boosting foods for kids" found at http://www.sheknows.com/living/articles/808306/brain-boosting-foods-for-kids.

So if your teen is feeling tired after school and having a hard time getting started on homework, it could be what they are eating. Switch out the sugary snacks and serve up nuts, power bars, peanut butter, jerky, and other protein dense foods to fuel their brain.

Homework Helpers to Build Time Management Skills

While the Personal Homework Profile is intended to help you and your student create a holistic approach to homework, here are some specific homework helpers and tips. Again, the details and specifics of how you will use any of these will depend on your student. They are meant simply as suggestions. So, pick and choose the ones that resonate with your teen!

Schedule Daily Homework Time. Even if your teen has "no homework" on any given evening, he or she can use that time to get ahead in their reading, make up missed work, work on an extra credit project or begin reviewing notes for a test. This consistency will help keep your student on track.

Simplify the Supplies. As best you can, simplify the amount of supplies your student uses, and they will automatically save time. It's easy for them to get overwhelmed by the amount of papers, homework sheets, handouts, etc. that take over their school life. Use a master binder, accordion file or individual notebooks or folders to corral papers. The more places your child has to look for something, the more time it will take them to find. Even if your child's teacher has a specific set of requirements, work with the teacher to create an organizing system that is easy to use and maintain and works best for your child.

Create a School Stuff Storage Station. How many times have you seen your 13-year old waste 20 minutes looking for a pencil sharpener when it is time to do homework? Gather all the supplies they need for homework at the beginning of the school year (think colored pencils, reinforced paper, calculator, etc.) and fill a clear and portable box. Make sure to label with their name AND a list of all the supplies in the box. This easy solution takes the "I don't know where it is" mantra out of the equation! Remember to make a box of supplies for EACH of your children. Different ages need different supplies!

Organize your Child's Environment. It's hard to talk time management without mentioning organization. They go hand in hand. It is just as important to have their bedroom, study area or back pack organized as it is for them to have time management skills. Organizing these zones will help them stay on schedule and focused, and you will avoid the dreaded "I am looking for my vocabulary homework to hand in, and I have no idea where it is!"

Use a Timer. Devices such as timers and buzzers can help a student self-monitor AND keep track of time. For example, during quiet or reading time, a timer placed on a student's desk can help the student know exactly where the time is going and also help the student become aware of when transitions to other activities will take place.

Make a Homework Plan. Even if your teen is recording his homework in his planner, have him write out a to-do list for the night. Have him write them in order of how he will get them done AND estimate how much time it will take to complete each assignment. This will generally depend on the Personal Homework Profile for your teen. For some students, I suggest putting the hardest or longest task at the top and doing that one first when they have a "full tank of gas." They will feel a sense of accomplishment when having tackled the hardest "to-do" first. For those that truly procrastinate, I recommend doing the smallest and easiest task to get them started. For most, doing a combination of both is best.

My student Hannah loved to mix it up. She would start off with the easiest assignment to get herself going and then tackle the hardest assignment. When she was finished, she went back again to an easy one as a reward. No matter which method they choose, the most important thing is to make a plan. By actively committing to what they are going to do and when, they are more likely to accomplish what they committed to do.

Try Body Doubling. A "body double" functions as an anchor. The presence of another individual focuses a person and makes it possible for them to ignore distractions and keep them focused on their tasks. For example, if your teen is doing homework, you might work on a laptop or read a book either at the table with them or close by. You might even be nearby in your home office or kitchen. Remember Randy, my teen who needed to work at the kitchen table with his siblings close by? Their close proximity helped Randy stay anchored and get his work done. For high school and college students working in a school library can provide the same benefits.

Work in bursts. Encourage your teen to work in bursts. We all struggle to maintain attention when doing activities that don't interest us. Working intensively for a short period of time and then taking a break helps you learn more. Studies show that students remember and focus more when they take breaks between study sessions instead of studying straight through for an extended period.[7]

Get Active. Put "energy" into their homework tasks by having your student stand up to read or walk the dog while they review their notes. My son is always studying scripts and memorizing lines. He paces with his book in hand, using it as a reference to check as he memorizes it. As we discussed with Rachel, research shows that the more we move, the more our brain "lays down its learning."

---

7 "6 Tips to Fight Distractions and Get Homework Done!" found at http://www.additudemag.com/adhd/article/print/8394. html.

CHAPTER 6

Is There A "Cure" for Procrastination?

Of all the concerns I hear from parents, procrastination is at the top of everyone's list, and with good reason.

Over 50% of the general population procrastinates in some form or another. For students, this number is over 70%![8] I am a firm believer in allowing students to create their own time profile and preferences for getting things done, but sometimes allowing them to work on their own schedule can create an environment for procrastination. Research—and there is a lot of it—shows that students who are serious procrastinators typically make more mistakes in their work and feel more stress.[9]

Why is procrastination so prevalent?

For some, the act of getting started is just too difficult and overwhelming. The task feels too big or the assignment seems too vague. For others, it's the lack of

---

8 Steel, Piers, "The Nature of Procrastination: A Meta-Analytic and Theoretical Review of Quintessential Self-Regulatory Failure" found at http://studiemetro.au.dk/fileadmin/www.studiemetro.au.dk/Procrastination_2.pdf.

9 Id.

a "time sense" or knowing how long something takes to get done. I'm sure many of you have heard your teen say he can complete a six-page research paper in less than 2 hours. Then there are those who like to work under pressure. Without that deadline, they just can't muster enough energy to start. Do you have a teen at home who proclaims "I'll get to it…later?" And of course, "later," either never arrives or arrives too late.

Procrastination Can Be Mood Based

Regardless of how procrastination manifests itself, it is important to have an understanding of what leads someone to procrastinate in the first place. There has been a lot of research conducted in the last few years that shows that procrastination is "mood based." In a recent Wall Street Journal article, Dr. Timothy Pychyl, an associate professor of psychology at Carleton University in Ottawa, Canada and a researcher on this topic, explained that often, procrastinators attempt to avoid the anxiety brought on by a tough task with activities aimed at "repairing their mood."[10] This pattern, which he calls "giving in to feel good," makes procrastinators feel worse later on when they have to face the consequences of not getting done what they needed to.

So how would this theory play out with a student?

Let's say your teen comes home from school and has that pesty English paper to write. Instead of sitting down and getting to work, he thinks, "I need to do something that will put me in a good mood before I can

---

10 "To Stop Procrastinating, Look to Science of Mood Repair" found at http://www.wsj.com/articles/SB1000142405270230393 3104579306664120892036.

deal with that miserable paper." So, he plays a few video games or logs onto Facebook, and before you know it, two hours have gone by. Is his mood any better? Maybe, but even so, that good feeling will be short-lived. In fact, soon thereafter your teen will likely feel worse than when he walked in the door initially because of all the wasted time. Now, there are three fewer hours to work on that paper, and your student is facing the prospect of incurring the wrath of a teacher or parent.

Help Your Teen Get Stuff Done

We're all wired to put things off, BUT we also have the capacity to override that tendency. Here are some essential strategies for helping your teen overcome his procrastination tendencies:

Provide Clear Expectations

Teens need a clear idea of what needs to be done and the steps that must be taken to get there. So, whether it is working on a science project or cleaning up in the backyard, a teen will perform better if expectations and timelines are specific. Taking the time to make sure your teen understands each task and what it will take to complete them will eliminate confusion later on.

Break Larger Projects Into Small Achievable Tasks

I can't stress this point enough. Breaking things down into manageable parts makes working toward them less overwhelming but, it ALSO provides multiple opportunities for realizing the success that comes from finishing each part. With success comes a sense of accomplishment, a feeling of "I can do it!" So, instead of telling your teen to clean up the backyard, break that task down into steps, such as (i) empty flower pots into waste bags, (ii) bring waste bags to side of house for garbage pickup, (iii) place empty flower pots and gardening tools in garage, and so on. It is much easier for teens to wrap their brains around completing each of these steps which makes it easier for them to initiate and get started.

Assign "Due Dates" and Schedule Appointments for Each Task

If the task is school-oriented, with a deadline, you can help your teen assign "due dates." Work backwards to figure out how much time she will need to accomplish each task. Assign deadlines to complete each one and schedule them as regular assignments so your teen will know when to work on them. This step is critical. Most students will know to get homework that is due the next day done. However, while making time for long term assignments and projects can be more challenging, it is critical to time management success.

Use a Timer

This is one of the simplest, yet most powerful tools we can use to keep on track. Setting aside a predetermined amount of time to work can help a teenager to stay on task during that time period. If someone only has an hour to do what normally takes two, they are more likely to get in gear and stay there. Have your student use a timer that actually shows time moving which will provide a visual cue to help manage time.

Make Getting Started Simple

Whatever your teen gets started on should be so easy or so small that success will be guaranteed. Research shows that even the worst procrastinators can improve by creating a very small goal to begin with. One math problem, one vocabulary word, one page to read, or one paragraph to write. You get the idea. Chances are that once your teen gets started, he will do another math problem, read another page, or write another paragraph. The dread that drives procrastination is almost always exaggerated. So once your teen sees that "it's not that bad," he will usually have the confidence to keep on going.

Create Their Happy Place

I believe everyone needs to create positive energy around their tasks to get motivated, and, to that point, environment is key. Paint your daughter's bedroom orange if that is her favorite color and that's where she studies. Have your son's favorite foods on hand when it's time to get down to homework, or purchase new pens or school supplies if that truly makes your student happy. Create an environment that will provide your teen with motivating enthusiasm. I like to think of it as a natural caffeine boost.

Reward Your Teen

I'm a big believer in rewarding behavior that is positive instead of punishing behavior that isn't. Decide what behavior you are going to focus the reward on and come up with an incentive for your teen. If the goal for your teen is to start homework on time each night, give a reward each time that goal is met. Make sure you ask your teen what she wants to work towards. It's essential to have input to make the rewards effective.

Forgive Them

We get super angry with our teens when they procrastinate over and over again. Research shows that all that negativity is making the problem worse! So, instead of getting on their case about it, forgive them. You'll be better for it and so will your teen.

CHAPTER 7

How Do I Get My Teen Out the Door in the Morning?

D o your mornings look something like this?

"I have two kids (14 and 16). Both have difficulty waking up in the morning. They turn their alarms off and go back to sleep. When they finally do get out of bed, they spend endless amounts of time deciding what to wear or in the bathroom. More than once they have gotten dressed in the car. They eat whatever they can grab, since by the time they are finally ready, we are already late. They just don't have any sense of time in the morning! And by the time I drop them off, I am exhausted and frustrated."

If you are the parent of a teen, you already know that getting through the typical morning routine can be very stressful. Getting your teen up, dressed, fed, and prepared for school and out the door in the morning is a huge challenge for everyone. There is a big emotional tug of war going on here as well.

On one hand, you want your teen to be independent and get out the door on his own. On the other hand, you also fear that if you leave your teen alone he will never make it to school. It really doesn't have to be that way. Before leaving your teen to navigate the morning alone, concrete and consistent routines need to be established.

Difficulties Waking up

The first challenge is helping your teen get up in the morning. I can't stress enough the importance of a good night sleep. There is no magic bullet here. In most cases, the better the night's sleep, the easier it is to wake in the morning. However, there are those teens that have trouble waking up even when they do get a good night's sleep.

How can you get your teen up in the morning? Purchase alarm clocks that have extra loud bells or buzzers. No snooze features! Avoid setting your teen's clock to music. Music tends to become white noise and lulls them back to sleep. Also, while the most natural place to put an alarm clock is next to the bed, for the teen that has problems waking up, the nightstand is the worst spot imaginable. Place the clock as far away from your teen's bed as possible. That will force her to actually get out of bed to turn the alarm off. Once out of bed, the odds that she will get moving increase exponentially. Setting multiple alarms is also a great strategy. If your teen has her own bathroom or there is one next to her room, place one in there as well. This will get her in the bathroom before she even realizes what happened.

Does your teen wake up irritable AND hungry? In my house, we call it "*hangry*." Your teen's brain is in desperate need of "brain fuel" to get him out of that cranky or angry state. Offering protein-rich foods within the first 15 minutes of waking can really help your teen get going. If your teen doesn't want to eat first thing, prepare a protein shake or purchase a premade one he can grab on the way out the door. A few sips can do wonders for regulating their mood.

Preparing For the Day Begins the Night Before

A smooth morning is usually the result of proper planning and preparation, and that begins the night before. My rule of thumb is that anything that CAN be done the night before to prepare for the next day SHOULD be done.

Choose Clothes

Have your teen pick out all his clothes, which means everything from accessories to shoes and coats. Have him take all the clothing out of his bedroom and leave it in either the kitchen or the bathroom that is closest to the kitchen. By removing clothing from your teen's bedroom, you are also removing the temptation to switch outfits and therefore the opportunity to lose track of time.

Shower the Night Before

We all know our teens love their bathroom time! They tend to get "lost" in the shower with no sense of urgency. By encouraging your teen to shower the night before you will cut down on morning prep time significantly, and your teen may be able to gain a little extra sleep as well.

Get Breakfast Prepped and Ready
Set out dishes and utensils. Premeasure oatmeal or pour out cereal. Place yogurt within easy view in the refrigerator or protein bars where your teen can easily see them. You will shave minutes off the morning routine if you have breakfast ready to go the evening before. This goes for lunch as well. Have your teen pack and prepare his school lunch before going to bed.

Set Up a Launching Pad
A launching pad is a designated place in the home where your teen's stuff that goes back and forth to school is kept. It's the place where backpacks, library books, instruments, gym sneakers, etc., should be stored every day. A launching pad takes the stress of packing up for the day out of the equation! Remember to pick the most trafficked area that your student uses. It could by the front door or even outside their bedroom.

Make a Reminder Checklist So Your Teen Doesn't Forget Anything
List items such as cell phones, keys, lunch bags, homework, musical instruments, sporting equipment, etc. Tack it to a cork board or write it directly on a wipeboard to make changes easy.

Have Your Family Meeting
If you need to go over the day's schedule or after school plan with your teen, have your meeting the night before.

Having a calm and relaxed conversation at night will minimize forgetfulness the next day.

Creating a Successful Morning Routine

Time Your Tasks

A common mistake parents make in creating morning schedules is being unrealistic about how long certain tasks take their children to complete. To improve the morning routine, keep a time log for about a week or two noting how long each task takes your teen to accomplish. This information will help you plan the mornings better and establish how much time everyone actually needs to get out the door stress free.

Set it to Music

Listening to music can invigorate the morning routine. If your teen needs an energy boost to get going in the morning, don't be afraid to blast the tunes. In my house, the first thing my husband does when he gets downstairs in the morning is to turn on the stereo. Nothing puts a smile on my face in the morning faster than hearing my son come out of the bathroom singing whatever song is playing because then I know he's up, moving and energized. For younger teens, you can use music as a game. Play "who can get done before the song ends" to move your child through their morning tasks.

Beat the Clock

If your teen seriously dawdles in the morning try **"BILL BOARDING."** First, place an analog clock in each room of your house that your teen uses (Yes, even the bathroom!) so he can see the "sweep" of time. Hang a dry-erase board or giant post-it note next to the clock with the time written down that your teen needs to be OUT of that room. So for example, if he needs to be out of the bathroom at 7:30am, then post that on the board. Seeing the time move alongside what time he needs to be moving to the next activity will help motivate your teen and keep him on track.

Provide "Body Doubling"

Most children and even teens need help moving through their morning routine. So instead of yelling to get dressed or eat breakfast, try body doubling them. This might mean your teen gets dressed in the bathroom near the kitchen while you are in the kitchen finishing breakfast preparations or sip your cup of coffee with your teen while she sits to eat breakfast. Remember, getting out the door in the morning is our priority, not theirs.

Give Choices

Cede control whenever you can. Does your son want to brush his teeth at the kitchen sink? Does your daughter want to put on her jacket in the car? Maybe that's not what you would do or even want them to do, but why not let them? As long as your teen is moving through the morning routine, give him as much control as possible.

CHAPTER 8

How Can I Manage the Technology Distractions?

Do you know what FOMO is? If you don't, you should. Over half of the teenagers (ages 13-17) living in the United States today have it and the numbers are growing every day.[11]

"FOMO" is the **F**ear **O**f **M**issing **O**ut—on something more interesting, more exciting or just plain better than what you're currently doing and to combat that anxious feeling, you've got to constantly stay connected with others lest you miss something important or exciting.

I'll let one of my student clients explain it even further:

"I feel like I need to be available to my friends 24/7 or I'll miss out on something or worse, not be included. It makes me so anxious that I constantly check my phone even while doing my homework."

While we know that technology is tough for all of us to ignore (I should have counted how many times I

---

11 "Teens and the Fear of Missing Out (FOMO)" found at http://www.ikeepsafe.org/balancing-screen-time/teens-and-the-fear-of-missing-out-fomo/.

checked my email while writing this book!), the FOMO factor is, perhaps not surprisingly, extra intense during the middle and high school years. In this day and age, teens aren't just juggling their day-to-day commitments. They also watch their social lives 24/7 fly by on social media while experiencing heart wrenching dread that they'll miss out on something that will threaten their social status. And I'm not exaggerating.

So how do you know if your teen has FOMO? Ask yourself these questions:

- Is your teen active on Facebook, Instagram, or Twitter?

- Do they email, text and/or use social media at key times during the day, such as right after waking or before going to sleep?

- Do they keep their phones next to them during meals, while watching television or even in the bathroom?

- Is their phone never more than 6 inches away while doing homework or studying?

- And do you know if they are texting friends or checking social media accounts during class time or at school?

The technology distractions don't stop there.

One of the most frequently asked questions I get is how to curb video and computer game use. Parents complain to me that their teens are spending countless hours playing Mindcraft, World of Warcraft, or games on the X-Box or PS4 like Call of Duty or Madden, either alone or with friends. One could argue—and I know my teen definitely does—that playing these games has a social component. Regardless, go on line, pick up a parenting magazine, or just listen to the conversation at the next table; the discussion and debate on screen usage in teens is everywhere.

The point of this chapter is NOT for me to tell you whether your teen should be on social media or use computer screens. It's not even to tell you how much is appropriate. What I am saying is that if your teen's technology use is seriously affecting her home life and academic performance—if technology is affecting her ability to get stuff done—then she probably is spending too much time on it. If that is the case, your teen is not managing the time she uses the technology well. Helping to devise strategies to manage the time your teen is using technology IS the point of this chapter. So how do you do that?

Create a Plan

The first step is to talk to your teen, not in an accusatory, lecturing manner, but in a real, two-sided discussion about the challenges of focusing on what needs to be done while acknowledging the real pull of social media.

How does their technology affect their homework? Why is it so hard to turn off a phone? What do they do to ignore distractions? Hopefully, a dialogue will produce some good strategies.

I had a student client who had an awful time getting started on her homework each night. She just couldn't turn off her phone herself. When her mom suggested that she give the phone to her to hold on to while she studied, she jumped at the chance. "Now I can tell my friends that it's my parents fault I can't have my phone while I study instead of me." Obviously an easier solution then most, but it was born out of open communication.

I had another student, Sarah, who had a very difficult time limiting her computer usage. Her parents established a "Black Out Hour" or "Quiet Hour" in the home each night where all screens including her parents were turned off. Sarah could use this time to read and do assignments that didn't require electronics. This hour was truly non-negotiable and helped Sarah budget her screen time appropriately.

What about the teen that needs the computer to check homework or work on assignments? Again, there is no magic bullet. I suggest you set up the computer in a common space, not in a bedroom, to discourage playing games, chatting with or emailing friends, or surfing the Internet for fun during study time. And that goes for the telephone too!

All teens need some type of plan to map out the appropriate times for computer screens and social media. Explain to your teen that when she truly "unplugs" and concentrates, she will actually find herself more focused and productive. And most importantly? She will save time! Multitasking doesn't really work. When you're trying to accomplish two different tasks, each one requiring some level of attention, multitasking falls apart. Your brain just can't take in and process two separate streams of information at the same time. It actually makes you less efficient.

Having your teen learn how to manage her time and the decision making regarding tech time will be crucial for future success. Having a serious strategy session with your teen to create a healthy relationship with social media and technology can be a priceless time management lesson.

Media Distraction Plugins

If you feel that your teen seriously lacks the self-control to monitor his tech usage, there are dozens of apps and settings that can be installed directly on a computer. These programs allow you to set time periods during which your teen will have no access to the Internet at all or block certain websites from his computer during certain parts of the day. As with any technology, it changes daily, but here are a few of the most common media distraction plug-ins available:

Freedom (macfreedom.com):

Freedom works by disabling a computer's internet connection for the time period you specify. When Freedom is running on your teen's computer, she will not able to get online at all. Freedom makes no permanent changes to the computer. If your teen needs to get back online, say, to do research for a paper, she can just reboot the computer.

Anti-Social (anti-social.cc):

Rather than blocking the Internet in its entirety, Anti-Social automatically blocks all known time-robbers for a set period of time. Sites that are off limit include Twitter, Facebook, YouTube, Vimeo, and more.

Self-Control (selfcontrolapp.com):

With Self-Control, you can block out distracting websites for a set amount of time. It is truly customizable in terms of which sites you can block and for how long. No amount of browser restarts or computer reboots will stop it. However, rather than completely disabling the entire Internet, you can selectively decide which sites are OK or not.

Cold Turkey (getcoldturkey.com):

Cold Turkey is specifically designed for students to help them focus and stay on-track. Not only does it block common websites and programs, but you can also program it to block certain computer games as well.

CHAPTER 9

Can I Really Survive Teaching My Teen Time Management Skills?

Absolutely! But here's the long answer.

Time management issues effect most teens—those with learning differences and attention deficits as well as the most able learners.

I can't recall how many stories I've heard from my friends about their teens that—at their heart—were about time management. Tales of research papers being written the night before they were due, struggles getting out the door in the morning or endless hours spent on electronic devices, when examined closely are all centered on time management issues. And, unfortunately, these issues—and parents' efforts to address them with their teens—tend to create a very toxic environment in the household.

While this is common, it doesn't have to be. Parents and teens are really on the same page when it comes to time management—they just don't realize it! Because as much as teens will insist "It's not a problem" or "I've got everything under control," it's the rarest of teens that will say they enjoy the all-nighters, the last-minute rushes or the incessant arguments in the house. Teens want to do well. And succeed. They just want to do it in their own way. If we start with those understandings then we can get on the path to success.

So is every one of my clients a success story? No. But most of them are. And here are three important lessons I have learned along the way from working with hundreds of families over the years.

First, for a student to be truly successful, a parent's involvement is critical. And by involvement, I don't mean that parents need to turn into helicopters, hovering over their child each and every minute. I mean that a parent can't just call for outside help—or throw this book on their teen's nightstand—and think they've done enough. Granted your degree of involvement will depend on your teen; but whether you are offering support and guidance from the sidelines or providing scaffolding every step of the way, creating the proper, nurturing, positive environment in which your teen can reinforce what they have learned is essential for them to master these skills.

As you go through the book, work with your teen on some of the concepts and ideas I've detailed and experiment with them. Keep in mind that you're not only trying to get your teen through middle or high school or bring some order to your chaotic household—you're providing your child with life skills that will serve her for many years to come.

Second, often these skills are thought of as something to be taught once, mastered and moved on. Or in my house what we call "one and done." And that could not be further from the truth. The fact of the matter is that time management skills are a learned skill. And to master any learned skill one must PRACTICE, PRACTICE, PRACTICE. There is no magic elixir here. Consistency is key. Trust me, I know. I meant what I said that finding ways to untangle my son's world became my passion. And it still is today. A day does not go by that I don't grab an opportunity to make any situation a teaching moment. "Eli, if you need to be at rehearsal at 5:15, what time do you need to leave the house?" "How are you going to remind yourself to leave at 5:00?" And on it goes.

Lastly, what if your teen won't let you help him? For any of these strategies to truly work, your teen needs to be on board. And willing to work with you. Truthfully, parents aren't always the best teachers for their child. Whether it's emotions getting in the way or the fact that you don't feel you have the necessary skills to teach your teen, don't be hard on yourself. A coach or tutor may be the answer. How many times have you said, "He won't listen to me, but he'll listen to his coach/teacher/tutor!" In my years of practice, even the students who were the most resistant to my help came around. It just took time.

So don't get discouraged. Trust yourself and your teen, keep working at it and try different approaches until you find what works. Learn together. Use this book as a resource to refer to again and again. Hopefully you will find something new and useful each time you do. Don't expect instant results. Keep the lines of communication open. And remember, you are all on the same team.

This is only the beginning. Enjoy the journey! I am honored to be a part of it.

Resources

There are so many resources available that it is impossible to list them all. I have rounded up my favorite websites, resources, products and apps that I use to help my students organize their time and space and stay on track.

Books/Websites

Train Your Brain for Success: A Teenager's Guide to Executive Functions, Randy Kulman, PhD, published by Specialty Press.

That Crumpled Paper Was Due Last Week, Ana Homayoun, published by Perigee Books.

Organizing the Disorganized Child: Simple Strategies to Succeed in School, Martin L. Kutscher, MD and Marcella Moran, published by William Morrow Paperbacks.

Homework Made Simple, Ann K. Dolin, M.Ed, published by Advantage Books.

Smart but Scattered, Peg Dawson, EdD, and Richard Guare, PhD, published by The Guilford Press.

Order Out of Chaos®: orderoochaos.com. The Time Map found on page 33 and the Project Planning Guide found on page 40 can be printed out in pdf format from www.orderoochaos.com.

GreatSchools: greatschools.org

Time Management Magazine: timemanagementmagazine.com.

LifeHacker: lifehacker.com.

Academic Planner

Order Out of Chaos® "Academic Planner: A Tool For Time Management®": orderoochaos.com.

Electronic Organizers

Skoach: skoach.com. An online task planning and scheduling tool.

myHomework: myhomeworkapp.com. An online homework scheduling and organization tool.

Keep Track of Time

Watchminder: watchminder.com. A watch with programmable vibrating reminders to help students stay on task and focus.

TimeTimer: timetimer.com. Displays the passage of time visually. Available as an app too!

Pomodoro Timer Lite: play.google.com. Focus for 25 minutes and the timer signals it's time for a break.

FocusTime: focustimeapp.com. Allows you to set work and break intervals.

Focus Booster: focusboosterapp.com. Provides digital visual cues to keep track of time.

Mark-My-Time: mark-my-time.com. A bookmark-style timer for timing independent reading.

Stay On Track/Set Reminders

30/30: itunes.apple.com. Make a list and give yourself a time allotment to complete each task.

iCalendar: itunes.apple.com/Google Calendar: play.google. com. Both sync with cell phones, allowing you to schedule online and to set reminders by email or text.

Wunderlist: wunderlist.com. Ideal for keeping track of homework, projects and schedules.

StayOnTask: play.google.com. This app will periodically "check in" with you to make sure you are doing what you are supposed to be doing.

Study minder: studyminder.com. Homework organizer that keeps track of work times.

Wake Up

Wake N Shake: wakenshakeapp.com. You have to vigorously shake your iPhone to wake up.

I Can't Wake Up!: play.google.com. You do eight wake-up tasks before the alarm is silenced.

Clocky and Tocky: nandahome.com. These alarm clocks jump off your nightstand and roll around your room while playing your favorite mp3s.

Time Management Tools

Post-It Calendar and Picopad Wallet: amazon.com. Customizable wall calendar and post it note wallet.

Analog Clocks: amazon.com.

Evernote: evernote.com. Students can capture all their documents in one convenient place.

Coaching for Teens and College Students

JST Coaching: jstcoaches.com

Edge Foundation: edgefoundation.org

Institute for Challenging Disorganization: challengingdisorganization.org

Organizing Products

Case-it binders: caseit.com. The best all-in-one master binder on the market! My favorite is the Dual-101 with two sets of rings.

Duo 7-Pocket Accordion File Binder: wayfair.com. An all-in-one binder that combines a 3-ring binder with an accordion folder.

Delta Planners' Student Sleeves: deltaplanner.com. An oversized vinyl pouch perfect for holding student supplies.

Graphic Organizers: Studenthandouts.com. Visual outlines to help students organize information.

Presentation Boards: staples.com. Three-sided table top display boards can be used during homework time for privacy if working in an open space.

Locker Supplies: lockerbones.com. Customizable locker shelves that help keep your student organized.

Yoga Ball Chairs: Yogaballchairs.com. Great alternative to a regular chair especially for those students who tend to fidget while doing homework.

Could It Be Something Else?

If you sense that your child is more time challenged or disorganized than others his age, it's worthwhile to consider that something else may be going on. Discuss your concerns with your child's doctor, teacher, school counselor or therapist. Remember, you are your child's best advocate. Parents always know if something is not quite right.

Here Are a Few Resources to Explore:

Late, Lost, and Unprepared: A Parents' Guide to Helping Children with Executive Functioning, Joyce Cooper-Kahn, Ph.D and Laurie Dietzel, Ph.D, published by Woodbine House.

Children and Adults with Attention Deficit Disorder: chadd.org. Reliable information and support.

ADDitude Magazine: additudemag.com. Strategies and support for ADHD and Learning Differences.

National Center for Learning Disabilities: ncld.org. Comprehensive information, materials and research.

LD Online: ldonline.org. A superb resource including useful articles on multiple issues.

About the Author

Leslie Josel is the Principal of ***Order Out of Chaos®***, an organizing consulting firm specializing in student organizing and chronic disorganization. Launched in 2004, ***Order Out of Chaos®*** offers organizing, time management and coaching services; provides family education and ADHD resources as well as teleclasses, webinars, videos, and products to hundreds of families.

Leslie is a graduate of the JST Coach Training Program for teens and college students with ADHD. She is a Golden Circle member of the National Association of Professional Organizers (NAPO) and earned her Chronic Disorganization and Hoarding Specialist certificates from the Institute for Challenging Disorganization (ICD).

Leslie is the creator of the award winning ***"Academic Planner: A Tool for Time Management®,"*** a student planner that helps middle and high schoolers develop and master time management skills.

A respected resource on ADHD and Executive Functioning in students, Leslie speaks and conducts workshops nationally to parent and educator groups on a variety of issues and topics facing students today, including The Matan Institute, National Ramah Camping

Commission, and the Institute for Challenging Disorganization. Leslie has also been featured in national broadcast and print media such as the Hallmark Channel's "The Better Show," "Conversations in Care" radio, The Associated Press, Family Circle Magazine, and Educational Dealer Magazine.

Also known nationally as an expert on chronic disorganization and hoarding issues, Leslie has appeared on many episodes of TLC's hit television show, "Hoarding: Buried Alive", the Cooking Channel's television special, "Stuffed: Food Hoarders" and "dLife-TV." She is also the co-author of the award winning "The Complete Diabetes Organizer: Your Guide to a Less Stressful and More Manageable Diabetes Life" (Spry, 2013).

To sign up for the Order Out of Chaos® monthly newsletter, read their weekly blog, access free videos, resources and information or learn more about Leslie, visit their website at www.orderoochaos.com. Active on social media, you can also find Leslie on Twitter @ orderoochaos, as well as Pinterest, YouTube and at www.facebook.com/orderoutofchaos.

82196138R00050

Made in the USA
Columbia, SC
29 November 2017